Songs from a Lost
SOUL

Songs from a Lost
SOUL

by

A.G Wilson

Novel Name: *Songs From a Lost Soul*

Typeset by: digitalatdeunique@gmail.com

First Printing: 2018

Cover By: GRAPHIC STUDIO

ISBN : 978-93-87131-06-4

PAPER TOWNS PUBLISHERS
72, Vishwadham Colony, Niwaru Road, Jhotwara
Jaipur-302012
www.papertownsindia.com

This is dedicated to all of you.

Preface

There are perhaps many clichés that can be associated with poetry, and I am here to tell you that every one of them are true.

For no matter the many praises we place upon poetry can we fully appreciate the value it brings to our lives.

Perhaps Robin Williams said it best in the movie Dead Poets Society

Medicine, law, business, engineering, these are noble pursuits and necessary to sustain life. But poetry, beauty, romance and love. These are what we stay alive for.

I hope that this book adds beauty to your lives.

Acknowledgments

I am heavily indebted to many people who have showered me with love and support throughout, without which I wouldn't dare dream of the possibility of writing a poem much less a book of poems. Firstly, my thanks goes out to my friends, Mr. John Althaide and Mr. Niranjan Kumar, who on one tiresome evening sent me a poem reflecting the drudgery of the corporate world, and subsequently result in my first attempt at a poem, therefore, giving me that much needed push towards writing poetry.

Next, I would like to thank two teachers who took the time to sit down and appreciate my attempts at writing Ms. Ruth Manoj and Ms. Tasmiya Hussni. Perhaps I am at fault for not fully impressing upon you the impact your words of encouragement did have on me.

My parents, Mr. Wilson G and Ms Yessumonie Wilson, who have instilled in me a love and passion for books and reading, this is perhaps the single greatest gift in life that anyone could have perhaps given me, second only to your love and support of my hare-brained schemes.My brother, Mr. Abhishek G Wilson for the many times he has pitched in to contribute ideas, support and the tireless sharing of my work, Thank you!

A big thank you to Ms. Bhavana Sahai and Mr Sanjay Sahai for proof reading this ludicrous attempt of a book, and of course for the tons of delicious food showered on me while I was writing this book.

A special word of thanks to my colleagues at Christ Institute of Management (Lavasa) for your constant love and support, for your words of encouragement and wishes during my birthday celebration that I should publish a book soon. It has really pushed me to attempt this.

It would be amiss to not thank Ms. Jyothi Priya R, who has in particular been a constant source of support from the wordpress days.

Special thanks to Mr. Navin Victor for all the support on social media, I am undoubtedly in your debt for the shoutouts and support you have shown towards my work. A big thank you

From initiating the idea of getting onto Instagram right upto sharing poems that would help be become a better writer and giving me your inputs at regular intervals, no matter how harsh I might add, Thank you Ms. Elizabeth Matthew and Mrs. Gazala Amreen for your constant support.

A sincere thank you, to all of those who follow me on Instagram and have faithfully liked and shared my posts, and have offered me a lot of in particular, Ms. Unnati G Hunjan, Ms. Kavyashree, Mr Allan Ashish, Mr. Suraj Ramesh, Mr. Siddarth Chilukur, Ms. Amanda Bonnie, Ms. Torani Makana, and Mr Anandhu Bose, I am forever in your debt.

Contents

Part I: Romance

Beauty

There are those times when you come across someone who takes your breath away, and in that moment in time you cannot help but be lost in the moment.

As I stumble through these hallowed halls
Beauty does greet my gaze,
The songs of the trees,
The caress of the breeze
Fills mine heart with bliss
However, fair maiden
All of nature, as charming as she can be
None can compare to the beauty that adorns thee.

– A.G. Wilson

Always

This is a nod to Harry Potter fans, Severus Snape is perhaps the epitomy in the embodiment of what many would agree was love in perhaps it's purest form, protecting her son from harm no matter how great the price. He would eventually pay the ultimate price and sacrifice his life that Harry Potter would live. The poem is an imagination of the uniting of these two souls in the afterlife and she finally falls in love with him.

I gazed into his emerald eyes, as my life began to fade,
The scar across his forehead lies, a relic of that fateful day,
My vision blurs, and countenance fall
As the Dark Lord's curse upon me reign.

Distant memories pass me by, as the venom construes my soul
Perhaps the fading hope revived, that once again we may be whole,
Upon your face do I gaze, as once again I walk by your side

At long last do I see my love reflect within your eyes.
Many a song about me sung, of the days of yesterday,
An ode to undying love, which lived through none but pain,
Though these tales by men have writ

None of them may see
The truth about my life is naught what you perceive to be.
So gather round the fireplace young ones
And listen to this tale,
Gather around, brace yourself
For it is The Prince's tale.

– A.G Wilson

Always II

Into my arms like a dream she came
At long last, I feel her warm embrace
The emerald eyes that upon me gaze
Bear for me no contempt, nor hate.

The horrors of the past long forgotten
The smirch of a word through my anger begotten
Mudblood! I yelled in my rage and affliction
To banish the one who I loved in vain.

Gently caress my cheek did she
As my palm she held on lovingly
A single tear did blemish her face
As gratitude emanated through her careless grace.

Moony, Padfoot, Wormtail and Prongs
Their malignant ways did you wrong.
How could this debt I ever repay?
Tell me Sev! Ask away!

The price in life I had to pay
Was considered by many to be far too great
But in those last moments as upon your eyes I gazed
I realised I would do it all again
Through the heartache, through the pain
For you my love I will fall, Now and Always.

\- *A. G Wilson*

Always III

Lily:

Forgive me Severus, Perhaps you will,
Anguish in life and in death despair,
How great must this burden have been that you bear?

You dared to tempt the Dark Lord's bane
All for me, who you loved in vain
Forgive me Severus, I cannot understand
This ardent devotion for my son you have.

You are indeed a worthy one,
Perhaps the greatest among Slytherin's sons,
The Patronus you cast is of me
But it is you who me safely keeps.

Our journey now in lament will not end,
Together we walk once more in the night,
The hearts that were torn apart in life
At long last in death unite.

At long last did their journey unite,
The doe doth walk with the dark prince by his side,
Sleep well little ones, for the tale now ends,
Farewell until we meet again.

- A.G Wilson

Undying Love I

Death is perhaps one of the great mysteries of life, and it is always leaves a vacuum in the hearts of those who have lost someone, it is more painful when it is one of your parents. Sometime back a dear friend's mother passed away, and there was a sense of numbness that surrounded the air, there were no words I could say to express how truly sorry I was for her loss. This poem was an attempt to somehow try to perhaps reach out to my dear friend and remind her that her mother would always be watching over her no matter what.

Sleep well my child for i am here,
Fret not little one, shed not a tear,
In my loving care will you lay
Fear not! Do not be dismayed.

Sleep does she a little child
Fears cast away far and wide
A world of dreams bid her to haste
Yet the child clings on to her mother's waist.

Go forth! My child, arise! Awake!

Waste not a minute! Waste not a day!
The world is thine, and thou art mine
Fear not this day and walk your way

Burden not me oh my mother!
Ask another i pray!
The world is wicked with it's merry ways!
Let this child lay down and stay.

– A. G Wilson

Undying Love II

Come here my child, walk with me,

Look not the other way

Cast aside your fears and wipe your tears

And set your spirit free!

Fear binds your heart, and holds you near

Holds you close to what be dear

Open your eyes that you may see

The giants that your illusions purport to be

For you dear mother! I rise up today!

March upon the path, the giants to slay!

Be still! You demons, i shall not fear

For at my side is my mother dear.

Mountains bow down, and seas be tamed

Behind me lie my giants slain

Come forth dear mother!

Where hast thou gone?

Mine eyes search, but ye cannot see
Mine lips plead but ye do not hear
Where art thou dear mother
Stop these games i pray!

- A.G Wilson

Undying Love III

Behold! Dear child, search not in vain,
For in this realm I cannot stay
The time hast come to tune my harp
And to sing his glorious praise!

Walk on dear child! For you shall see
Your mother's love lies with thee.
Calm will i these petty storms
Crush adders on the way!
Walk with you through every storm
And guide you on the way!
Fear not my dear, cast aside thy fear
And walk thy graceful way
The ones we love, true and dear
Depart not from your heart!

Into your heart gaze oh dear soul
And know that this may be
That thou art mine and i am thine
Though none of them may see

I pray for you my dear child
With a heart steadfast and true
Go forth little one!
Waste not your time
For my love shall always be thine!

– A.G Wilson

Quotes

An eternity did I search in vain,
For the peace I found in you.

- A.G Wilson
©thesouthernbard

I want you to be a part of every chapter I write.

- A.G Wilson

©thesouthernbard

It has been years since I saw you last,
Yet the wounds you left,
remain scarred upon my soul.

- A.G Wilson
©thesouthernbard

How easily you set ablaze the beast that lies within.

- A.G Wilson

While you set out on your meaningless pursuit for love,
Life gazes at you longingly from afar.
Wondering how it feels to know your touch,
Longing to feel alive.

- A.G Wilson
©thesouthernbard

When I write the final chapter of my life,
Will I still feel your warmth on my chest?
As I pull you close for one last kiss.

- A.G Wilson
©thesouthernbard

I held you but for a moment,
And you left me with a lifetime of memories.

- A.G Wilson
©thesouthernbard

Your love rekindles the fire within my soul,
As through you I become whole.

- A.G Wilson
©thesouthernbard

The shadows of your memory haunts me, as I walk through these halls.

- A.G Wilson

Ever so gently do I feel your touch,
A breath so faint my falling spirit to renew,
When the bane of darkness does prey upon my heart,
You rejuvenate my countenance anew.

- A.G Wilson
©thesouthernbard

Like a withering leaf by the dew of morn,
Your touch my soul renews.

- A.G Wilson
©thesouthernbard

As I gaze upon this lost highway,
My soul reaches for you.
And for all the things that could›ve been.

- A.G Wilson

I found myself in the missing pieces of your soul.

- A.G Wilson

I gazed upon you longingly, in disbelief,
As finally you were in my arms where you belong.

- A.G Wilson
©thesouthernbard

And slowly the sparks turn to flame,

As I held you in my arms,

While night turned to day.

- A.G Wilson

It will always be you,
For when you hold me in your arms,
The world can do me no harm.

-A.G Wilson

You are the perfect symphony,
A bit of chaos,
With a touch of ecstasy.

- A.G Wilson

Gaze upon the stars my love,
And fly away with me.

- A.G Wilson
©thesouthernbard

Embrace yourself the way you are,
With all your scars and your rough edges,
Look not for validation through the eyes of another,
For all you need to know is that you›re beautiful.

- A.G Wilson
©thesouthernbard

Oh how I miss your warmth and the comfort of your skin.
The gentle beat of your loving heart to nourish this wounded soul within.

- A.G Wilson
©thesouthernbard

When you find someone who stirs the embers of your soul, hold on. It›s the gentle whisper of the universe bringing you closer to what you desire.

- A.G Wilson
©thesouthernbard

Before you there are no secrets to hide,
My solace, my comfort, my creed, my love!
I gave you my heart,
You redeemed my soul,
You are the peace that calms my spirit cold.

- A.G Wilson
©thesouthernbard

Breathe upon me your breath of life,
And show me what it means to feel alive.

-A.G Wilson
©thesouthernbard

I long for your warmth by my side,
To feel the rhythm of the day
Fade into the velvety night.

-A.G Wilson

My heart beats in harmony,
With the music of your soul.

- A.G Wilson
©thesouthernbard

A stranger rests in my arms,
where you once belonged.

- A.G Wilson
©thesouthernbard

If I were to show you the scars upon my heart,
Will you still come closer as I reach for your embrace.

- A.G Wilson
©thesouthernbard

Your light and not your beauty will shine through in your darkest hour.

- A.G Wilson

©thesouthernbard

Lovers by night and strangers by day,
How futile these games we play.

- A.G Wilson

Of all the things I could be,
I want to be yours.

- A.G Wilson

In your eyes I saw eternity,
And in your soul salvation.

- A.G Wilson

You bring solace to my soul amidst the scourge of war,
The burden on my shoulder I bear alone no more.

-A.G Wilson
©thesouthernbard

Across a thousand lifetimes,
Across a thousand souls,
I will always reach for you.

- A.G Wilson

Would it be a sin if I lost myself in the oceans of your soul?

- A.G Wilson

With a touch of alchemy,
You gave me a glimpse of eternity.

- A.G Wilson
©thesouthernbard

Her beauty reached out from the dark yonder
and immersed me in light.

- A.G Wilson

As you swayed to the rhythm of the beat,
You became my captor and my creed.

- A.G Wilson
©thesouthernbard

Though we are miles apart,
Know that my soul is yours.

- A.G Wilson
©thesouthernbard

How easy it is to fall in love,
When your hearts already beat as one.

- A.G Wilson
©thesouthernbard

Her broken soul looked to heaven and sought to fly again,
Could she be healed?
Or did she hope in vain?

- A.G Wilson
©thesouthernbard

When the journey of their days come to close,
They will meet once again,
One last time upon this earth to lay.
Under the starry skies converge.

- A.G Wilson

You reached out for me through the veil,
The shackles binding my heart begin to break.

- A.G Wilson
©thesouthernbard

No words I weave can compare to the Beauty that graces my eyes.

- A.G Wilson

©thesouthernbard

Marks of passion adorned my skin,
Yet I did not know love.

-A.G Wilson

The memory of you haunts me wherever I go,
The scars upon my soul console me why you had to go.

-A.G Wilson
©thesouthernbard

Gently your breath, my skin did caress,
As the magic that is you,
Took hold of my dreams.

-A.G Wilson
©thesouthernbard

As time does fade from my mind›s eye,
I realized you would too.

-A.G Wilson
©thesouthernbard

She always was an enigma to me,
Breathtaking, like a wildflower,
Drenched in summer›s rain.

- A.G Wilson
©thesouthernbard

Her touch was softer than the finest of silk,
But the fire in her soul is what ensnared me.

- A.G Wilson
©thesouthernbard

Open your mind and perhaps your heart,
Look through my eyes,
To see how beautiful you are.

- A.G Wilson
©thesouthernbard

If I knew that was the last time I›d gaze upon your face,
Would I have let you walk on without regret?
Or would I have said the things left unsaid.

- A.G Wilson
©thesouthernbard

Hold me close and never let go,
For darkness has held me captive for far too long.

- A.G Wilson
©thesouthernbard

I gaze upon the wild blue yonder,
Wistfully immersed in my thoughts,
I think back to the days of yesterday,
When you were safe in these arms.

- A.G Wilson
©thesouthernbard

Distant memories pass me by,
As this venom construes my soul,
Perhaps the fading hope revived,
That once again we may be whole.

- A.G Wilson
©thesouthernbard

The wintry cold on the darkest of nights,
Withers away by the warmth of your light.

- A.G Wilson
©thesouthernbard

In those last moments as upon your eyes I gazed,
I realised I would do it all again.

- A.G Wilson
©thesouthernbard

A room full of art looks empty without you.

- A.G Wilson

You judge me for not being in love,
I pity you, for what you define as love.

- A.G Wilson
©thesouthernbard

Together we walk once more in the night,
The hearts that were torn apart in life
At long last in death unite.

- A.G Wilson
©thesouthernbard

As I longed for dawn›s sweet embrace,
The kiss of darkness bid me to haste.

- A.G Wilson
©thesouthernbard

Into my arms like a dream she came
At long last, I feel her warm embrace
The emerald eyes that upon me gaze
Bear no contempt, Nor hate.

- A.G Wilson

Lovers lie gently under this grand canvas of old,
To wish upon a falling star,
as their fathers have before.

- A.G Wilson

In a world filled with chaos you bring peace unto my heart.

- A.G Wilson

At long last did their journey unite,
The doe does walk with the dark prince by her side.

- A.G Wilson
©thesouthernbard

Part II: Reflections

The Wait For Destiny I

There are those moments in life where you seek to put your past behind you and try to move forward in life. However, whatever the reason maybe you find yourself grasping at straws oftentimes doubting your decisions. This poem depicts the journey of the protagonist who is faced with two beings, a being of light and one of darkness. The conversation that ensues is captured in these verses.

There is a time that for us waits,
A call that will change your fate
Where will you be that fateful hour
Will you rise or watch from afar

Wondrous tales heard I of men
Who changed the face of our realm
Dared to reach for the mighty stars
While we stare in awe from afar

Many a time in reverence I stare
A world of despair does my heart bear
Bound am I by the chains of fate
Oh! can I reclaim this state?

My chains are broken! My burdens gone!
Is this the freedom that I so longed!
For truly the time to rise has come!
To ascend my throne and reclaim my crown!

"Be still dear boy, Walk not so quick
Walk with me, here hold my stick"
Perplexed am I by this horrid sight
Who is this man with his walking stick?

- A.G Wilson

The Wait For Destiny II

A grimace torments his face so young
He tries to speak but makes not a sound
A frown creases his face
A face that reveals the struggles of an entire race.

What a horrid apparition upon which I stare!
One soo young! Yet borne with despair
Who are you spectre? Why do you despair?

I am he who ye will be
The curse upon man that you want to see
Behold the scars upon my brow
For they are ones you forge on your own

His face was twisted with the burden of time
A heart that knew neither reason nor rhyme
A vacant gaze to reflect his soul
Is this what I become in my days of old?

A mighty light next to me came
A joyous creature shone forth through the veil

A spring in his step, mirth upon his lips
And charm that could melt the devil's pit

Who are you stranger? I ask of him.
Tell me true, what fills you to the brim.

- *A.G Wilson*

The Wait For Destiny III

Despite myself I smiled at his face,
Who are you stranger? Do tell me I pray!
He smiled and embraced me with the warmest of hugs
There you are O brother mine!
To meet you I have waited the longest time

Yet again he laughed at my puzzled gaze
I am you young man
Or are you me? I can never understand
Nonetheless this is you many years from now
You have lived your life to the fullest and how!

There is none you want from life no more
It has filled you with joy to the brim
You let yourself live atlast
Torn away from your horrid past

I look at him with dismay and look at the other
who grimaced with pain
How can both of you be me?
Why are you in shackles?
and why are you free?

The grimace turned into a smile so faint as
he looked to the other to explain
My boy we are both whom you can become
The question is who do you want to be?
The demons of the past haunt your soul
As you plea for the pain to hurt no more
However dear child can't you see
The demons are not real
They needn't be

Life is naught what happened to you
It is what you hold to be steadfast and true
Hold on to the demons and pain you will embrace
But hold on to love and joy you will be
Hold on to life and let me be
Let me show you all you can be

Take his hand said the grimace
Trust me it's true
These demons in your heart have no hold on you
The past has past and has no need to be
The chains you speak of depart and now you are free

I gaze upon their faces as they smile
The pain and misery are in me no more

They both embrace with their warmth and set me
upon a new day's dawn
I look on to the glorious horizon that beckons me near
And hold on close to my heart that is so dear.

- A.G Wilson

Humanity's Lair

Humanity has managed to take many strides in the fields of science and technology, however, for all our accomplishments we seem to have forgotten our compassion for those in need. This poem was inspired by a young child who was begging on the streets as she watched other children her age go past her to study at school.

I feel her hunger and her pain
As she looks into mine eyes in vain
For a morsel of food, Maybe a nickel or two
To get her by this rainy day.

Sorrow fills my spirit, as I glance back at her stare
Is this all I can do! Is there nothing I can do?
Can I not save her from this fate!

I toss her a buck, and pray for her luck
To calm my storming mind
And march away my spirit free
Yet my heart lies with the child

A crippling grief tears my spirit as I walk the other way,

A heart so helpless, a child left motherless
By the world's wicked ways.
Groomed by insolence, nurtured by intolerance
Awake not do we in the hour of humanity's need.

Consumed by fantasy, pushed on by reality
We turn away from her need.
We lay her bare cast not but a stare
And leave her as she lay,
Pronounce her judgment with a cruel air,
'That tis better for her this way!'

I hear a cry, I hear her plead as we walk through our mighty lives
'Heal me please I beg of ye, Are we not children of His Grace'
'Be still vile woman, back away from me!
I know not ye nor your Grace'

Is this what we are?
Is this who we be?
Anointed supreme! The chosen being?
To Lord o'er his mighty works,
Yet cower in fear, pretend to not hear
When she calls upon our name

You stand aloof in her hour of need
While crowds sing your praise
Yet the child lays bare with none to care,
And gazes in hope at humanity's lair.

- A.G Wilson

Memories

This poem dwells upon the various memories that lie dormant at the back of our minds, and how these long forgotten tales seem to get a new lease of life when given the right touch.

A bright new day greets me as I from slumber wake,
The birds render to me in glorious harmony,
A ballad my spirit to awake.

I gaze upon the wild blue yonder
Wistfully immersed in my thoughts
I think back to the days of yesterday
Though today they seem afar.

Strangers pass me by as I trudge upon this path of mine,
Wonder do I often of the tales they have to tell,
Will they speak of love long forgotten? And of how they fell?
Will they speak of the joys begotten? From a life lived well?
Tis strange is it not? The symphony of our worlds.
Innately unique and yet somehow converge.
Many of you from my mind's eye do fade,
Some more distinct, while others remain.

What new memories for us await?
As we this journey now undertake.
Whose paths are headed our way? And whose paths from us depart.
Memories are perhaps time's greatest gift,
or perhaps it's worst I cannot tell.

For while some memories illuminate the corners of our hearts,
Others seek to tear us apart.
In all nonetheless I await,
The songs that birds have to sing on yet another day.
Another journey ends while another begins.
In the end, memories are all that will remain.

- A.G Wilson

Hope

There are at times when the world around you causes you to lose faith in all that surrounds you, however, there are those rare moments that instils hope in you that no matter how far you may seem to fall from life, you must always hold onto hope.

Ever so gently do I feel your touch,
A breath so faint my falling spirit to renew,
When the bane of darkness does prey upon my heart,
You rejuvenate my countenance anew.

These demons from my past do emerge,
As I the world now I seek,
A world filled with unkind gifts
For they who are meek.

Yet then again when all hope seems lost,
There are a precious few,
They are not the best of men
Nor are they the best of you.

They greet me with a smile, they do,
And scars upon their brow,
Many a war waged have they,
Many a trial have they come to know.

Arm in arm we walk on then,
Upon this winding road,
These scars are but a remnant now
Of the sorrows that they knew.

Hope emanates from them as I gaze now into their soul,
Perhaps I was wrong to infer,
To be happy you need to be whole,
Yet here these warriors amidst me walk, they smile despite it all,
Therefore, now I walk jauntily amongst you all
Onwards on this winding road.

As the day begins it's demise,
The sun departs from the vale that lies amidst the skies.
The warmth of the day goes by, as the darkness embraced the skies.

My mind takes me back in time,
The old astronomer who lay to rest amongst the starry skies,
His soul will never in darkness set
For his love for God's mighty firmament is alive.

Lovers lie gently under this grand canvas of old,
Wish upon a falling star, as their fathers have before,
She raised her head to the skies, like a child lost in time,
The wonder of God's masterpiece is reflected in her eyes,
His gaze, however, did not for a moment waver,
For God's most perfect masterpiece lay not in the stars above,
But was gently cradled in the confines of his heart.
There was another, with a different tale,
Who under the vast expanse did lay,
Many were the years added unto his life,
A life complete with joy and strife.
He smiled gently as he watched them in sweet embrace,
And thought back to the days of his youth,
where he too did all the care in the world forsake,
It had been many a year since his sweetheart did depart,
Onto a journey that led her down a different path.
Before her journey began, they made a solemn vow
When the journey of their days come to close
They will meet once again,
Last time upon this earth to lay longingly in sweet embrace.
Many a journey under the night sky does converge,
Chapters of many writ under the same stars.
I wish you well on your journey today,
May peace and joy be the gifts you partake.
Write this story, and write it well,
May it hold true as the night casts her spell.

- A.G Wilson

A League of One

This poem was originally written for a play. The protagonist is a self-centred, egoistic, all powerful monster who declares to the world that they need to acknowledge him as their ruler.

From time immemorial to time evermore
You will bow down to the beast of yore
For in your eyes pretence i see
The demons of your past will never let you be
Corrupted in spirit, infected in your soul
You pretend to be noble, and claim to be more
Ha! You fool stay your tongue
You'd sell your own mother just for fun!
Desist your foolishness and the lies you speak
Remove this veil and come dance with me
gaze in my mirror and the truth you will see
The truth of who you really be

I am not the monster, Nor is he me
I am no saint, who will set you free
I am like none who hath come before

Nor will there be forever more

Feast your eyes all on me

For I am!

I am a league of one!

- A.G Wilson

A Breath of Freedom

When the vices that surround you decide to leave you or rather you decide to desert them in the pursuit of something greater. This poem is a caution against falling prey to these wayside distractions.

Like a withering leaf by the dew of morn
my soul now renews
a breath of life fills my lungs
with purpose now anew

The demon, the snare, the temptress and the imp
No more! no more! do I feel their nip!
Free at last! Their ship has sailed!
Behold now the truth may prevail.

Listen closely and listen quick
Beware these demons and their tricks
Ever enticing with their wayward tongues

Ever eager to fill you with filth and scum
Heed not these creatures

They prey on the weak
They have no sympathy for they who are meek
Vice their friend and malice their ally
Innocence the meal upon which they pry
Beware these monsters and their ways
Beware for they come in many ways
These monsters wear masks to hide their ways
And enchant us to go their way
Beware dear children
Watchful you must remain
And resist these fools and their wicked ways.

- A.G Wilson

The Monster

Oftentimes we look upon monsters as creatures that are deformed and are from the depths of hell itself, however we seem to forget that the most vicious of monsters lie confined within the depths of our souls.

Behold my light shines brighter than a thousand suns
For I am, I am a league of one
The stars above so mighty and bright
Shine down on us, amidst the darkness of night
They speak, they sing, of things foregone
They echo tales of an era long gone
To undo the past and renew the future
We seek of naught but a sliver
Of hope, of rage, Of love and hate
Songs sung when the day is done
The minstrels sing till their harps undone
Many are the tales of warriors and kings
Many are the heroes of whom they sing
Thousands live and thousands have passed
Lived their lives like the grass and moss
There have been none like me before

Nor will there be for evermore
I am the monster and the monk
The demon before whom you bow
The beast of yore, the beast of now
The harvester of souls, the sinners son
The poet who sings upon his harp
The monster consuming the victors lark
To feast to dine on your sinful souls
I am a creature like none before
You wanted the saint
You molested the giver
Slain the friend and butchered the lover
Here I stand, this is all that remains
The masks of goodness stripped away
Gaze upon this face O man
This is what I really am
This is the beast that you now breed
This is the monster that you feed.

- A.G Wilson

The Night Sky

This poem was inspired by the velvety skies of lavasa as the day came to a close. The picturesque scenery of Lavasa and the beauty that surrounds you inevitably takes your breath away, this was one of those days that you have no say in the matter and just have to take it all in.

As the day begins it's demise,
The sun departs from the vale that lies amidst the skies.
The warmth of the day goes by, as the darkness embraced the skies.

My mind takes me back in time,
The old astronomer who lay to rest amongst the starry skies,
His soul will never in darkness set
For his love for God's mighty firmament is alive.

Lovers lie gently under this grand canvas of old,
Wish upon a falling star, as their fathers have before,
She raised her head to the skies, like a child lost in time,
The wonder of God's masterpiece is reflected in her eyes,
His gaze, however, did not for a moment waver,
For God's most perfect masterpiece lay not in the stars above,
But was gently cradled in the confines of his heart.

There was another, with a different tale,
Who under the vast expanse did lay,
Many were the years added unto his life,
A life complete with joy and strife.

He smiled gently as he watched them in sweet embrace,
And thought back to the days of his youth,
where he too did all the care in the world forsake,
It had been many a year since his sweetheart did depart,
Onto a journey that led her down a different path.

Before her journey began, they made a solemn vow
When the journey of their days come to close
They will meet once again,
Last time upon this earth to lay longingly in sweet embrace.

Many a journey under the night sky does converge,
Chapters of many writ under the same stars.
I wish you well on your journey today,
May peace and joy be the gifts you partake.
Write this story, and write it well,
May it hold true as the night casts her spell.

- *A.G. Wilson*

Lost Soul

In the journey of life there are many things that we long for, this poem is the journey of a lost soul looking for himself

In a time and place that I thought I knew,
In a life where I've never lived
I'm looking for redemption
Through a God I've never seen
They say, have faith in your Father,
He'll guide you through the storm,
I plead Father please forgive me!
I can't do this anymore!
I'm just a lost soul on a voyage,
Heading on to unknown shores
Living through life's mighty onslaught
Living through the wild highs and their lows
They say that life ain't no bed of roses
Trust me "boy" I speak the truth
I ain't looking for no roses
All that I seek is the honest truth.

- A.G Wilson

Quotes

Will you give in to fear,
Or will you rise above it?
Is the price of courage too high to pay?
Or will you choose to take a stand.

- A.G Wilson
©thesouthernbard

Don’t let one memory stop you, from the beauty that lies ahead.

- A.G Wilson

Let not your past define you,
Hold on to the promise of tomorrow.

- A.G Wilson
©thesouthernbard

Seek the things that lie ahead of you,
Move forward in faith.

- A.G Wilson

Take a moment to appreciate the beauty that surrounds you. It is all you need to see how beautiful you are.

- A.G Wilson

©thesouthernbard

Learn to smile, despite it all,

Everything you ever wanted will come to pass.

- A.G Wilson

©thesouthernbard

Trust yourself and be patient,
The earth shattering things that bother you today,
Will soon be a distant memory.
Just trust yourself and be true to who you are,
And watch the universe bring it all together.

-A.G Wilson
©thesouthernbard

Embrace your scars, wear them proud,
Let them remind you of how far you've come.

-A.G Wilson
©thesouthernbard

It is in our deepest darkness that light shines it's brightest.

- A.G Wilson

You were born to soar amidst the skies,
Yet you allow yourself to be tamed by society's lies.
What more will it take for the phoenix to rise from the ashes?

- A.G Wilson
©thesouthernbard

It's not by your thoughts,

but by your actions that history will judge you.

How will you choose to be remembered?

- A.G Wilson

©thesouthernbard

It's been you all along. While you've been waiting for the love of your life to rescue you.

You have ignored the truth that you already know.

It's you, it's always been you all along.

So stop waiting for someone else to define your happiness and allow yourself to become everything you've ever wanted to be.

- A.G Wilson

©thesouthernbard

Become just a little bit kinder,
A little more empathetic,
A little more loving,
And a lot more thankful,
And watch on patiently with a smile,
As heaven becomes a place on Earth.

- A.G Wilson
©thesouthernbard

Heaven lies not in the mystic skies,
Nor the stars that shine at night.
It lies within your soul,
To guide you to the light.

- A.G Wilson
©thesouthernbard

Trust your heart oh dear soul,
And watch your deepest desires unfold.

- A.G Wilson
©thesouthernbard

Don’t hide your imperfections,
That’s where your beauty lies.

- A.G Wilson
©thesouthernbard

Cradle your heart oh child of mine,
Let it hold strong and true,
Amidst these storms of hate and wrath,
Let love see you through.

- A.G Wilson
©thesouthernbard

What is this strength that courses through my veins?
A breathe of life, of hope renewed,
The burden and taunts of yesterday,
No more does my spirit break.

- A.G Wilson

These scars are but a remnant now,
Of the sorrows that I knew.
The lessons of the last remain,
As the mystery of this tale unfurls.

-A.G Wilson
©thesouthernbard

Memories are perhaps time's greatest gift,
or perhaps it's worst, I cannot tell.

- A.G Wilson
©thesouthernbard

The symphony of our worlds is a beauty unto herself,
Innately unique and yet somehow converge.
Many of you from my mind's eye do fade,
Some more distinct, while others remain.

- A.G Wilson
©thesouthernbard

I wish you well on your journey today,
May peace and joy be the gifts you partake.
Write this story, and write it well,
May it hold true as the night casts her spell.

-A.G Wilson
©thesouthernbard

Unleash your spirit! set it free!
Let it soar! like it was meant to be,
Let fear bind your heart no more.

-A.G Wilson
©thesouthernbard

The Beast came forth in dark embrace,
To dance our unholy duet once again.

- A.G Wilson
©thesouthernbard

Some memories warm the corners of our heart,
While others seek to tear us apart.
On which of these do you choose to dwell?
Think hard dear reader and choose them well.

- A.G Wilson

©thesouthernbard

Dream did I to stand amongst them,
The dreamers, the lovers, the best of men!
Are these the musings of a delusional fool,
And do I dare dream in a world so cruel.

- A.G Wilson
©thesouthernbard

His face was twisted with the burden of time,
A heart that knew neither reason nor rhyme,
A vacant gaze to reflect his soul,
Is this what I become in my days of old?

- A.G Wilson

When destiny calls you near,
To dance amongst the stars,
Where will you be that fateful hour?
Will you rise? Or will you fall?

- A.G Wilson
©thesouthernbard

Beauty lies all around you,
If you but, choose to see.

- A.G Wilson
©thesouthernbard

Though there maybe trouble on the way,
Lose not your heart, nor your way,
For through the dark forest of the night,
Lies the guiding spirit of light.

- A.G Wilson
©thesouthernbard

In the end when the song is sung,
And memories are all that remain,
Will you regret the things that were,
Or that from which you refrain?

- A.G Wilson
©thesouthernbard

Author Profile

Ashish G Wilson is a poet or at least considers himself one, whether he is or not I leave it to you to decide. He works as an assistant professor at Christ Institute of Management, Lavasa, However, his heart has always belonged to the arts.

He was a script writer at Barefoot Productions and won the award for best script in 2016. More recently he has taken to Instagram going by the name 'thesouthernbard' where he shares poetry. And now has decided to dabble in poetry, which of course seems self-explanatory as you are reading this on the back of a book.